TAKE THIS JOB AND................

Donald Gorbach

Copyright © 2017 by Donald Gorbach

All rights reserved.

ISBN-10 1979252408
ISBN-13 978-1979252409

"NO SIR. I SAID PIRATE SHIP.
WHY IN THE WORLD WOULD I CALL YOU
A PIECE OF SHIT?"

— ANONYMOUS

REALITYGREETINGBOOKS.COM

www.ingramcontent.com/pod-product-compliance
Lightning Source LLC
Chambersburg PA
CBHW050214230526
45470CB00001B/379